Nations Of Africa

Speedy Publishing LLC
40 E. Main St. #1156
Newark, DE 19711

www.speedypublishing.com

Copyright 2014
9781635011135
First Printed October 28, 2014

Africa Facts:

Africa is the world's second-largest and second-most-populous continent.

Africa Facts:

At about 30.2 million km2 (11.7 million sq mi) including adjacent islands, it covers six percent of the Earth's total surface area and 20.4 percent of the total land area.

Africa Facts:

With 1.1 billion people as of 2013, it accounts for about 15% of the world's human population.

Africa Facts:

The continent is surrounded by the Mediterranean Sea to the north, both the Suez Canal and the Red Sea along the Sinai Peninsula to the northeast, the Indian Ocean to the southeast, and the Atlantic Ocean to the west.

Africa Facts:

Africa's population is the youngest among all the continents; 50% of Africans are 19 years old or younger.

Africa Facts:

The continent includes Madagascar and various archipelagos. It has 54 fully recognized sovereign states ("countries"), nine territories and two de facto independent states with limited or no recognition.

Africa Facts:

Algeria is Africa's largest country by area, and Nigeria is the largest by population.

Africa Facts:

Africa, particularly central Eastern Africa, is widely accepted as the place of origin of humans and the Hominidae clade (great apes), as evidenced by the discovery of the earliest hominids and their ancestors, as well as later ones that have been dated to around seven million years ago, including Sahelanthropus tchadensis, Australopithecus africanus, A. afarensis, Homo erectus, H. habilis and H. ergaster – with the earliest Homo sapiens (modern human) found in Ethiopia being dated to circa 200,000 years ago.

Africa Facts:

Although it has abundant natural resources, Africa remains the world's poorest and most underdeveloped continent, the result of a variety of causes that may include corrupt governments that have often committed serious human rights violations, failed central planning, high levels of illiteracy, lack of access to foreign capital, and frequent tribal and military conflict (ranging from guerrilla warfare to genocide).

Africa Facts:

Arabic is spoken by 170 million people on the continent, followed in popularity by English (130 million), Swahili (100), French (115), Berber (50), Hausa (50), Portuguese (20) and Spanish (10).

Africa Facts:

Over 90% of soils are unsuitable for agriculture and only 0.25% has moderate to low potential for sustainable farming.

Africa Facts:

Megafauna like giraffe, zebra, gorilla, hippopotamus, chimpanzee and wildebeest are unique to the continent and only found here.

Africa Facts:

The Serengeti (Tanzania) hosts the world's largest wildlife migration on Earth with over 750,000 zebra marching ahead of 1.2 million wildebeest as they cross this amazing landscape.

Africa Facts:

The Nile River is the longest river in the world with a total length of 6,650 kilometres. Lake Malawi has more fish species than any other freshwater system on earth.

Africa Facts:

Almost 40% of adults in Africa are illiterate.

Africa Facts:

Africa is the world's second driest continent (after Australia). The Sahara is the largest desert in the world and is bigger than the continental USA.

Africa Facts:

Africa is the most centrally located of all of the continents with both the prime meridian (0 degrees longitude) and the equator (0 degrees latitude) passing through it.

Africa Facts:

Islam became a prominent influence in North Africa by the seventh century A.D. and spread into sub-Saharan Africa through trade routes and migration. The population of North Africa is still considered widely Muslim today.

Africa Facts:

Egypt is the most popular tourist destination in Africa, attracting around 10 million visitors per year.

Africa Facts:

The oldest literate civilization in Africa is the Pharaonic civilization of ancient Egypt. Historical records date the rise of the Egyptian state to about 3300 B.C. and the fall from influence at 343 B.C., making it one of the world's oldest and longest-lasting civilizations.

60115242R00030

Made in the USA
Lexington, KY
26 January 2017